D1140573

SAY IT WITH A *Cupcake*

SAY IT WITH A *Cupcake*

SUSANNAH BLAKE

with photography by
Martin Brigdale

RYLAND
PETERS
& SMALL

LONDON NEW YORK

Senior Designer Toni Kay

Commissioning Editor Julia Charles

Production Hazel Kirkman

Art Director Leslie Harrington

Publishing Director Alison Starling

Food Stylist Linda Tubby

Prop Stylist Helen Trent

Indexer Hilary Bird

Notes

• All spoon measurements are level unless otherwise specified.

• All eggs are medium unless otherwise specified.

• Ovens should be preheated to the specified temperature. If using a fan-assisted oven, cooking times should be reduced according to the manufacturer's instructions.

• When using the zest of lemons or limes in a recipe, try to find organic or unwaxed fruits and wash well before using.

First published in the United Kingdom
in 2009 by Ryland Peters & Small
20–21 Jockey's Fields
London WC1R 4BW
www.rylandpeters.com

The recipes in this book were first published
by Ryland Peters & Small in *Cupcakes* and
Cupcake Heaven.

Text copyright © Susannah Blake 2009
Design and photography copyright
© Ryland Peters & Small 2007, 2008, 2009

All photography by Martin Brigdale except:
Carolyn Barber page 63; David Brittain page 36;
Peter Cassidy page 16; Chris Tubbs page 45;
Polly Wreford pages 29 and 41.

10 9 8 7 6 5 4 3 2 1

ISBN: 978-1-84597-913-3

A CIP catalogue record for this book
is available from the British Library.

Printed and bound in China

Contents

Baking the perfect cupcake

The great thing about baking cupcakes is that the ingredients and equipment required are basic. The techniques are generally simple and you need only the bare kitchen essentials to be able to rustle up the most professional-looking sugary creations to give as gifts.

Although there are many variations on the classic cupcake, most cupcake mixtures are based on four basic ingredients: butter, sugar, eggs and flour. Other ingredients such as chocolate, nuts, dried fruit and other flavourings, such as vanilla and grated lemon zest, may then be added to the mixture to add texture and flavour. For the best results, always use unsalted butter for cupcakes. For creamed mixtures, where the butter and sugar are beaten together, the butter should be left at room temperature until soft. The most common sugar for making cupcakes is caster sugar, but other sugars and sweeteners (such as honey) may also be used, all of which will add their own unique taste and texture. Eggs enrich cakes but also bind the ingredients together and are best used at room temperature. The eggs used in the recipes in this book are medium. Most cupcakes use self-raising flour or plain flour with a little baking powder to help them rise.

Quantities are important when baking cakes and using the wrong proportions of ingredients can lead to disappointing results. So make sure you have a set of accurate weighing scales, cups and spoons. The easiest way to make cupcakes is to bake them in cupcake tins, which usually have six to 12-cup shaped holes. For the prettiest effect, line them with paper cases before filling with cake mixture. As well as standard cupcake tins, you can also find mini-cupcake ones, which some of the recipes in this book use.

Whether your oven is gas or electric is unimportant. Some ovens have hot spots, and some cook faster than others, but as you get to know your own oven, you'll know whether you need to turn the cupcake tin round partway through baking to ensure evenly browned and risen cakes, or whether you'll need to adjust the cooking time.

Decorating your cupcakes is where the fun really begins! Simple or sophisticated, plain or indulgent. From the simplest glacé icing to swirls of rich buttercream – the options are endless.

Icings and frostings

Prettily coloured, sugary sweet icings and frostings that you can drizzle, spoon, swirl or pipe on top of cupcakes add a whole new dimension. Melted white or dark chocolate, or a glacé icing made from icing sugar and lemon juice are probably the simplest and are perfect for spooning or drizzling. Buttercreams, cream cheese frostings, chocolate ganaches, whipped cream and creamy custards are more indulgent and excellent for swirling and piping.

Fondant icing, which can be bought ready-made and ready-to-roll from the supermarket, is perfect for making sophisticated, professional-looking cakes. White icing can be splashed with a little food colouring, then kneaded to incorporate the colouring, rolled out, cut into rounds and draped over cupcakes to give a silky smooth finish to which decorations can then be added.

Sprinkles and other decorations

Once you've frosted or iced your cupcake, you can leave it plain, but it's even more fun to add decorations. A glacé cherry or a single brightly coloured sweet placed in the centre of the cupcake can be stunning. But there are also delightful coloured sugar sprinkles that you can scatter all over frosted cakes – from hundreds and thousands to tiny sugar shapes, such as hearts, stars and flowers. Other decorations include sugar and rice paper flowers, gold and silver dragées, edible sparkles and even birthday candles and firework sparklers that you can light at the table. Supermarkets and kitchen shops are full of fabulous decorations that are perfect for decorating cupcakes. Don't be afraid to let your imagination run wild!

Cupcake cases

There are many different types of pretty cupcake cases available. You can find them in supermarkets and kitchen shops and they come in a fabulous array of colours and designs. Look out for pretty pastels or bright colours, elegant floral patterns, fun prints such as footballs for boys, or

lovehearts for Valentine's Day. There are
shiny metallic cases, too – gold, silver and
other colours, or even stripes and spots.
There really is no end to the choice
out there! When giving cupcakes as
a gift, present them in cardboard or
cellophane boxes tied with ribbon
or in an attractive cake tin.

HAPPY BIRTHDAY

Birthday Surprise!

THESE DECORATE-YOUR-OWN-CUPCAKES ARE ALWAYS
A HIT AT A BIRTHDAY PARTY – WITH KIDS AND GROWN-UPS
ALIKE! EVERYONE WILL ENJOY GETTING CREATIVE AND
TRYING TO PRODUCE THE MOST OUTLANDISH CUPCAKE.

Preheat the oven to 180°C (350°F) Gas 4.

Beat the butter and sugar in a bowl until pale and fluffy,
then beat in the eggs, one at a time. Sift the flour and
cocoa powder into the mixture and fold in.

Spoon the mixture into the paper cases and bake in the
preheated oven for about 17 minutes until risen and a skewer
inserted in the centre comes out clean. Transfer to a wire
rack to cool completely.

To decorate, beat the butter until soft, then add the icing
sugar and milk and beat until smooth and creamy. Divide
the icing among three bowls. Add a few drops of food
colouring to each one and stir well to make a vibrant lilac,
yellow and green. Spoon into serving bowls.

Arrange the cakes on a plate and put the decorations in
individual bowls alongside the bowls of icing. Let the kids
or other guests decorate their own cakes.

115 g unsalted butter,
at room temperature

115 g caster sugar

2 eggs

115 g self-raising flour

1½ tablespoons cocoa powder

TO DECORATE

175 g unsalted butter,
at room temperature

450 g icing sugar, sifted

2 tablespoons full-fat milk

lilac, yellow and green
food colouring

brightly coloured candies,
such as dolly mixture,
Smarties and Jelly Tots

coloured sprinkles such as
hundreds and thousands,
sugar flowers and edible
coloured balls

*a 12-hole cupcake tin,
lined with paper cases*

MAKES 12

DELIGHTFULLY GIRLY, THESE GORGEOUS, SPARKLY
CUPCAKES ARE JUST PERFECT TO BAKE FOR ANY
YOUNG GIRL'S BIRTHDAY CELEBRATION.

Sweet Sixteen

115 g butter,
at room temperature

115 g caster sugar

2 eggs

115 g self-raising flour

1 teaspoon vanilla extract

2 tablespoons full-fat milk

TO DECORATE

about 6 clear red or pink
boiled sweets

185 g icing sugar, sifted

1 egg white

lilac food colouring

edible sparkles and edible
silver balls

*a 12-hole cupcake tin,
lined with paper cases*

MAKES 12

Preheat the oven to 180°C (350°F) Gas 4.

Put the butter and sugar in a large bowl and beat until
pale and fluffy. Beat in the eggs, one at a time. Sift over the
flour and fold in, then fold in the vanilla extract and milk.

Spoon the mixture into the paper cases and bake in the
preheated oven for about 17 minutes until risen and a skewer
inserted in the centre comes out clean. Transfer to a wire
rack to cool completely.

To decorate, leave the sweets in their wrappers and tap with
a rolling pin to break into large pieces. Set aside. To make
the icing, gradually beat the icing sugar into the egg white
until smooth and creamy, then beat in a few drops of food
colouring until the desired colour has been achieved. Spread
the icing on top of the cakes. Pile a little heap of boiled
sweet 'jewels' in the centre of each cake and sprinkle with
edible sparkles and silver balls. Let set slightly before serving
or packing.

Twenty One Again

THESE CUTE LITTLE PEANUT-FLAVOURED CAKES FILLED
WITH A BLOB OF FRUITY JAM ARE JUST PERFECT FOR THE
BIG KID IN ALL OF US. THEY MAKE GREAT MINI-DESSERTS
FOR A BIRTHDAY DINNER PARTY – JUST REMEMBER TO
WARN EVERYONE THAT THEY CONTAIN PEANUTS IN CASE
ANYONE IS ALLERGIC TO THEM.

Preheat the oven to 180°C (350°F) Gas 4.

Beat the butter, crunchy peanut butter and sugar together
in a bowl until pale and fluffy, then beat in the eggs, one
at a time. Sift the flour into the mixture and fold in.

Spoon dollops of the mixture into the foil cases and flatten
slightly with the back of a teaspoon, making a slight indent
in the centre. Drop about ½ teaspoon jam in the centre of
each indent. Top with the remaining cake mixture. Bake in
the preheated oven for about 18 minutes until risen and
golden. Transfer to a wire rack and leave to cool completely.

To decorate the cakes, put the smooth peanut butter and
mascarpone in a bowl and stir to combine, then stir in the
icing sugar until smooth and creamy. Swirl the frosting on
top of the cakes and sprinkle with edible balls. Pop a candle
in each cake, if using.

60 g unsalted butter,
at room temperature

60 g crunchy peanut butter

115 g caster sugar

2 eggs

115 g self-raising flour

2 tablespoons raspberry
or strawberry jam

TO DECORATE

3 tablespoons smooth
peanut butter

4 tablespoons mascarpone

50 g icing sugar, sifted

edible gold balls

12 candles (optional)

*a 12-hole cupcake tin,
lined with foil or paper cases*

MAKES 12

THESE GROWN-UP CUPCAKES ARE THE ULTIMATE
INDULGENCE – MOIST, CRUMBLY SPONGE WITH JUICY
RASPBERRIES AND A DRIZZLE OF KIRSCH, SMOTHERED IN
CREAMY CUSTARD AND TOPPED WITH FRESH FRUIT. THEY
MAKE A LOVELY BIRTHDAY TREAT FOR A SPECIAL FRIEND.

Best Friend's Birthday

115 g unsalted butter,
at room temperature

115 g caster sugar

2 eggs

115 g self-raising flour

140 g fresh raspberries,
halved

TO DECORATE

1 tablespoon kirsch

60 ml double cream

125 ml fresh custard

200 g raspberries and
redcurrants, or other berries
of your choice

*a 12-hole cupcake tin,
lined with paper cases*

MAKES 12

Preheat the oven to 180°C (350°F) Gas 4.

Beat the butter and sugar together in a bowl until pale
and fluffy, then beat in the eggs, one at a time. Sift the flour
into the mixture and fold in, then fold in the raspberries.

Spoon the mixture into the paper cases and bake in the
preheated oven for 18 minutes until risen and golden and
a skewer inserted in the centre comes out clean. Transfer
to a wire rack to cool.

To decorate, prick each cupcake all over with a skewer and
pour ¼ teaspoon kirsch over each one, allowing it to soak
into the cake. Whip the cream, then fold in the custard and
spoon on top of the cakes. Top each cake with raspberries
and redcurrants, or berries of your choice. These cupcakes
are fragile so take great care when serving or packing them.

Boyfriend's Birthday

THESE SOPHISTICATED CHOCOLATE-MOCHA CUPCAKES
MAKE THE PERFECT BIRTHDAY TREAT FOR THE MAN IN
YOUR LIFE. SERVE WITH A GOOD STRONG CUP OF COFFEE.

Preheat the oven to 180°C (350°F) Gas 4.

Put the chocolate in a heatproof bowl set over a pan of gently
simmering water. Do not let the bowl touch the water. Leave
until almost melted, then set aside to cool slightly.

Beat the butter and sugar together in a bowl until pale
and fluffy, then beat in the eggs, one at a time. Stir in the
melted chocolate and cocoa powder. Sift the flour into the
mixture and stir in, then stir in the coffee, followed by the
coffee beans.

Spoon the mixture into the foil cases and bake in the
preheated oven for about 20 minutes until risen and a skewer
inserted in the centre comes out clean. Transfer to a wire
rack to cool.

To decorate, beat the butter, icing sugar and coffee together
in a bowl until pale and fluffy. Spread the mixture smoothly
over the cakes and sprinkle with grated chocolate.

100 g dark chocolate,
chopped

150 g unsalted butter,
at room temperature

150 g caster sugar

2 eggs

2 tablespoons cocoa powder

100 g self-raising flour

2 teaspoons instant coffee,
dissolved in 1 tablespoon
boiling water

40 g chocolate-covered
coffee beans

TO DECORATE

100 g unsalted butter,
at room temperature

200 g icing sugar, sifted

2 teaspoons instant coffee,
dissolved in 1 tablespoon
boiling water

dark chocolate, finely grated

*a 12-hole cupcake tin,
lined with foil or paper cases*

MAKES 12

TRUE ROMANCE

Marry Me?

THESE SEDUCTIVE CHERRY-STUDDED CHOCOLATE
CUPCAKES ARE SPIKED WITH KIRSCH AND TOPPED
WITH FRESH CREAM – SIMPLY IMPOSSIBLE TO RESIST!

Preheat the oven to 180°C (350°F) Gas 4.

Put the chocolate in a heatproof bowl set over a pan of gently simmering water. Do not let the bowl touch the water. Leave until almost melted, then set aside to cool slightly.

Beat the butter and sugar together in a bowl until pale and fluffy, then beat in the eggs, one at a time. Beat in the melted chocolate, then stir in the almonds. Sift the flour and cocoa powder into the mixture and fold in, followed by the kirsch and glacé cherries.

Spoon the mixture into the paper cases and bake in the preheated oven for about 20 minutes until a skewer inserted in the centre comes out clean. Transfer to a wire rack to cool.

To decorate, put the chocolate in a heatproof bowl. Heat the cream in a saucepan until almost boiling, then pour over the chocolate and leave to melt for about 5 minutes. Stir until smooth and creamy, then stir in the kirsch and leave to cool for about 1 hour until thick and glossy. Spread the frosting over the cakes, top with a blob of whipped cream, a glacé cherry and a few chocolate shavings. Serve immediately.

90 g dark chocolate, chopped

115 g unsalted butter, at room temperature

115 g caster sugar

2 eggs

2 tablespoons ground almonds

150 g self-raising flour

1 tablespoon cocoa powder

2 tablespoons kirsch

50 g glacé cherries, halved

TO DECORATE

100 g dark chocolate, finely chopped, plus extra chocolate shavings

100 ml double cream

1 tablespoon kirsch

whipped cream, to top

12 glacé cherries

a 12-hole cupcake tin, lined with paper cases

MAKES 12

THESE RICH, DECADENT CHOCOLATE-ORANGE CUPCAKES, TOPPED WITH FRAGRANT ROSE PETALS, ARE THE PERFECT CHOICE WHEN ROMANCING A PASSIONATE CHOCAHOLIC.

Love Me, Love Me Not...

75 g dark chocolate, chopped

85 g unsalted butter, at room temperature

115 g caster sugar

2 eggs

3 tablespoons crème fraîche

115 g self-raising flour

1 tablespoon Grand Marnier

TO DECORATE

100 ml double cream

100 g dark chocolate, finely chopped

fresh rose petals, gently washed and patted dry

a 12-hole cupcake tin, lined with paper cases

MAKES 12

Preheat the oven to 180°C (350°F) Gas 4.

Put the chocolate in a heatproof bowl set over a pan of gently simmering water. Do not let the bowl touch the water. Leave until almost melted. Remove from the heat.

Beat together the butter and sugar until pale and creamy, then beat in the eggs, one at a time. Stir in the crème fraîche, then sift the flour into the mixture and fold in. Stir in the melted chocolate, followed by the Grand Marnier.

Spoon the mixture into the paper cases and bake in the preheated oven for 18 minutes until risen and a skewer inserted in the centre comes out clean. Transfer to a wire rack to cool.

To decorate, gently heat the cream until almost boiling, then pour over the chopped chocolate and leave to melt for about 5 minutes. Stir until the chocolate has melted, then refrigerate for 20–30 minutes. Beat until thick and glossy, then spoon on top of the cakes. Top each cake with a perfect rose petal to serve.

Be My Valentine

THESE DELIGHTFULLY FLIRTATIOUS CAKES FILLED WITH
A ZESTY LEMON CREAM AND FRESH RASPBERRIES ARE
GREAT FUN TO BAKE FOR VALENTINE'S DAY.

Preheat the oven to 180°C (350°F) Gas 4.

Beat the butter and sugar together in a bowl until pale and
fluffy, then beat in the eggs, one at a time. Sift the flour into
the mixture and fold in, then stir in the lemon zest and juice.

Spoon the mixture into the paper cases and bake in the
preheated oven for about 18 minutes until risen and golden
and a skewer inserted in the centre comes out clean. Transfer
to a wire rack to cool.

To decorate, use a sharp, pointed knife to remove a deep
round from the centre of each cake, about 3 cm in diameter.
Slice the raised bit off each piece of cored-out cake so that
you are left with a flat disc. Using the mini heart-shaped
cookie cutter, cut a little heart out of each disc.

Combine the crème fraîche and lemon curd in a bowl,
then fold in the raspberries. Spoon the mixture into the
hollowed-out cakes, then top with the hearts. Dust with
icing sugar just before serving.

115 g unsalted butter,
at room temperature

115 g caster sugar

2 eggs

115 g self-raising flour

grated zest and freshly
squeezed juice of ½ a lemon

TO DECORATE

80 ml crème fraîche

1 tablespoon good-quality
lemon curd

60 g fresh raspberries

icing sugar, for dusting

a 12-hole cupcake tin
(with heart-shaped holes
if you can find one), lined
with paper cases

a mini heart-shaped
cookie cutter

MAKES 12

Happy Anniversary

THESE SPECTACULAR DIAMOND-ENCRUSTED CUPCAKES
ARE PERFECT TO TAKE TO AN ANNIVERSARY PARTY. A SPICY
GINGER SPONGE IS TOPPED WITH A TANGY LIME ICING,
MAKING THEM A SOPHISTICATED TREAT.

115 g unsalted butter,
at room temperature

115 g caster sugar

2 eggs

115 g self-raising flour

3 pieces of stem ginger in
syrup, drained and chopped

grated zest of 1 lime

TO DECORATE

about 6 clear mints

2½ tablespoons freshly
squeezed lime juice,
plus extra as required

200 g icing sugar, sifted

blue food colouring

edible clear sparkles

*a 12-hole cupcake tin,
lined with foil or paper cases*

MAKES 12

Preheat the oven to 180°C (350°F) Gas 4.

Beat the butter and sugar together in a bowl until pale and
fluffy, then beat in the eggs, one at a time. Sift the flour into
the mixture and fold in, then stir in the ginger and lime zest.

Spoon the mixture into the foil cases, then bake in the
preheated oven for about 17 minutes until risen and golden
and a skewer inserted in the centre comes out clean. Transfer
to a wire rack and leave to cool completely.

To decorate, leave the mints in their wrappers and tap with
a rolling pin to break into pieces. Set aside.

Put the lime juice in a bowl, add the icing sugar and stir until
smooth. Add a little more lime juice as required to make a
spoonable icing. Add a couple of drops of food colouring
and stir in to achieve a pale blue colour.

Spoon the icing on top of the cakes. To decorate, pile a little
heap of mint 'diamonds' on each cake and sprinkle with
edible sparkles.

WHO WANTS TO EAT A HEAVY SLICE OF FRUIT CAKE
WHEN THEY COULD HAVE THESE DELECTABLY LIGHT
AND DELICATE VANILLA-FLAVOURED CUPCAKES INSTEAD!

Wedding Day

Preheat the oven to 180°C (350°F) Gas 4.

Beat the butter and sugar together in a bowl until pale and fluffy, then beat in the eggs, one at a time. Sift the flour into the mixture and fold in. Stir in the vanilla and the milk.

Spoon the mixture into the paper cases and bake in the preheated oven for about 18 minutes until risen and golden and a skewer inserted in the centre comes out clean. Transfer to a wire rack to cool.

To decorate, carefully fasten a piece of lace ribbon around each cake. Put the egg white in a large bowl, then beat in the sugar until thick and creamy. Beat in the lemon juice to make a thick, spoonable icing.

Spoon the icing onto the cakes, then top each one with a flower. The icing hardens quite fast, so work quickly as soon as you've made the icing.

Note: you can use larger or smaller muffin tins and cases to make a variety of sizes as these look very effective when displayed on a tiered cake stand (as shown).

115 g unsalted butter, at room temperature

115 g caster sugar

2 eggs

115 g self-raising flour

1 teaspoon vanilla extract

2 tablespoons full-fat milk

TO DECORATE

white lace or organza ribbon

1 egg white

125 g icing sugar, sifted

½ teaspoon freshly squeezed lemon juice

white edible flower decorations

a 12-hole cupcake tin, lined with paper cases (see note)

MAKES 12

SEASONAL TREATS

Happy Easter

CHILDREN LOVE THESE LITTLE CHOCOLATE NESTS WITH
PRETTY PASTEL-COLOURED EGGS NESTLING INSIDE.
THEY'RE EASY TO MAKE AND KIDS WILL HAVE A GREAT
TIME HELPING TO DECORATE THEM.

Preheat the oven to 180°C (350°F) Gas 4.

Beat the butter and sugar together in a bowl until pale
and fluffy, then beat in the eggs, one at a time. Sift the
flour and cocoa powder into the mixture and fold in,
then stir in the milk.

Spoon the mixture into the paper cases and bake in the
preheated oven for 18 minutes until risen and a skewer
inserted in the centre comes out clean. Transfer to a wire
rack to cool.

To decorate, put the mascarpone, sugar and cocoa powder
in a bowl and beat together until smooth and creamy. Pop
a dollop of frosting on top of each cake.

Break the chocolate flake bars into shards resembling twigs,
then arrange them on top of the frosting to create 12 little
bird's nests. Finish off with three chocolate eggs in the
centre of each nest.

115 g unsalted butter,
at room temperature

115 g caster sugar

2 eggs

115 g self-raising flour

1½ tablespoons cocoa powder

2 tablespoons full-fat milk

TO DECORATE

150 g mascarpone

50 g icing sugar, sifted

1 tablespoon cocoa powder,
sifted

2–3 chocolate flake bars

36 sugar-coated chocolate
eggs (about 100 g)

*a 12-hole cupcake tin,
lined with paper cases*

MAKES 12

Merry Christmas

THESE LIGHTLY SPICED CRANBERRY AND PEAR CUPCAKES,
TOPPED WITH A RICH BRANDY BUTTER FROSTING, MAKE
A DELICIOUS TREAT TO BAKE AND ENJOY THROUGHOUT
THE FESTIVE SEASON.

60 g unsalted butter,
at room temperature

115 g caster sugar

2 eggs

115 g self-raising flour

½ teaspoon mixed spice

1 pear, peeled, cored
and finely diced

40 g dried cranberries

TO DECORATE

100 g unsalted butter,
at room temperature

150 g icing sugar, sifted

4 teaspoons brandy

about 36 fresh cranberries

12 small holly leaves
(optional)

edible gold balls

*a 12-hole cupcake tin,
lined with paper cases*

MAKES 12

Preheat the oven to 180°C (350°F) Gas 4.

Beat the butter and sugar together in a bowl until pale and
fluffy, then beat in the eggs, one at a time. Sift the flour and
mixed spice into the mixture and fold in, then stir in the
pear and cranberries.

Spoon the mixture into the paper cases and bake in the
preheated oven for about 18 minutes until risen and golden
and a skewer inserted in the centre comes out clean. Transfer
to a wire rack to cool.

To decorate, put the butter, sugar and brandy in a bowl and
beat together until smooth and creamy. Swirl the frosting on
top of the cakes, then decorate each one with two or three
fresh cranberries, a holly leaf, if using, and sprinkle with
edible balls.

Happy New Year

THESE STAR-STRUCK SPONGES MAKE A DELICIOUSLY LIGHT
ALTERNATIVE TO TRADITIONAL FRUIT CAKE – PERFECT
WASHED DOWN WITH A GLASS OF CELEBRATORY FIZZ.

Make the star decorations the day before you plan to make
the cakes. Roll out the fondant icing, then use the cookie
cutter to cut out 12 stars. Set aside and leave to dry overnight.

When ready to make the cupcakes, preheat the oven to
180°C (350°F) Gas 4.

Beat the butter and sugar together in a bowl until creamy,
then gradually beat in the egg, followed by the orange zest.
Sift the flour into the mixture and fold in, then stir in the
brandy, followed by the dried fruit and glacé cherries.

Spoon the mixture into the foil cases and bake in the
preheated oven for 14 minutes until risen and golden and
a skewer inserted in the centre comes out clean. Transfer
to a wire rack to cool.

To decorate, gradually whisk the sugar into 2 of the egg
whites in a bowl until smooth and creamy, then beat in the
lemon juice. Spoon the mixture over the cakes and scatter
over the silver balls. Leave to firm up slightly. Place the star
decorations on top of the cakes, brush with the remaining
egg white and sprinkle with edible sparkles.

60 g unsalted butter,
at room temperature

60 g soft brown sugar

1 egg

grated zest of 1 orange

60 g self-raising flour

1 tablespoon brandy

4 ready-to-eat dried figs,
chopped

25 g sultanas

70 g glacé cherries, halved

TO DECORATE

100 g pale blue or white
ready-to-roll fondant icing

350 g icing sugar, sifted

3 egg whites

2½ teaspoons freshly
squeezed lemon juice

edible silver balls

edible clear sparkles

a mini star-shaped cookie cutter

*a 12-hole cupcake tin,
lined with foil or paper cases*

MAKES 12

THESE SWEET, SPICY PUMPKIN CAKES, TOPPED WITH
CREAMY WHITE AND DARK CHOCOLATE COBWEBS,
ARE DEFINITELY A TREAT RATHER THAN A TRICK!

Happy Halloween

115 g soft brown sugar

120 ml sunflower oil

2 eggs

115 g pumpkin or butternut
squash flesh, grated

grated zest of 1 lemon

115 g self-raising flour

1 teaspoon baking powder

1 teaspoon ground cinnamon

TO DECORATE

150 g white chocolate,
chopped

25 g dark chocolate

*a 12-hole cupcake tin,
lined with foil or paper cases*

greaseproof paper

MAKES 12

Preheat the oven to 180°C (350°F) Gas 4.

Put the sugar in a bowl and beat in the oil and eggs. Fold in
the pumpkin and lemon zest. Sift the flour, baking powder
and cinnamon into the pumpkin mixture and fold it in.

Spoon the mixture into the foil cases and bake in the
preheated oven for about 18 minutes until risen and a
skewer inserted in the centre comes out clean. Transfer
to a wire rack to cool.

To decorate, melt the white and dark chocolates in separate
heatproof bowls set over pans of gently simmering water.
Remove from the heat and leave to cool for 5 minutes,
then spoon the white chocolate over the cakes.

Roll a square of greaseproof paper into a cone and secure it
with sticky tape. Spoon the dark chocolate into it and snip
off the tip to make a piping bag. Put a dot of chocolate in
the centre of each cake, then pipe three concentric circles
around the dot. Using a skewer, draw a line from the central
dot to the outside edge of the cake and repeat seven times
all the way round to create a cobweb.

Fireworks Night

WHETHER IT'S 4TH JULY, BONFIRE NIGHT OR BASTILLE DAY,
THESE SPARKLING ORANGE-FLAVOURED CAKES ARE JUST
THE THING TO SERVE WHEN THE NIGHT SKY IS EXPLODING.

Preheat the oven to 180°C (350°F) Gas 4.

Sift the flour, cocoa powder and bicarbonate of soda into a
large bowl. Add the sugar and mix to combine. Make a well
in the centre.

Combine the orange juice and zest, oil and vinegar in a jug
and pour into the dry ingredients. Quickly stir together until
combined – the mixture should be quite liquid and gooey –
then spoon it into the foil cases.

Bake in the preheated oven for about 15 minutes until risen
and firm on top and a skewer inserted in the centre comes
out clean. Transfer to a wire rack to cool.

To decorate, put the chocolate in a heatproof bowl. Heat
the cream in a small saucepan until almost boiling, then
pour it over the chocolate. Let melt for 5 minutes, then
stir until smooth and creamy. Leave to cool until thick and
glossy, then spread over the cakes. Sprinkle the frosted cakes
with tiny silver balls and stick a mini-sparkler in the centre
of each one. Light the sparklers just before serving.

115 g plain flour

3 tablespoons cocoa powder

½ teaspoon bicarbonate
of soda

50 g caster sugar

120 ml freshly squeezed
orange juice

grated zest of 1 orange

3 tablespoons sunflower oil

1½ teaspoons white wine
vinegar

TO DECORATE

100 g dark chocolate,
finely chopped

100 ml double cream

edible silver balls

12 mini-sparklers

*a 12-hole cupcake tin,
lined with foil or paper cases*

MAKES 12

FAMILY TIME

Baby Shower

THESE SUPER-CUTE VANILLA-FLAVOURED MINI CUPCAKES,
WITH THEIR PRETTY PASTEL TOPPINGS, ARE PERFECT FOR
SHARING WITH GIRLFRIENDS AT A BABY SHOWER.

Preheat the oven to 180°C (350°F) Gas 4.

Beat the butter and sugar together in a bowl until pale and
fluffy, then beat in the egg, a little at a time. Sift the flour
into the mixture and fold in, then stir in the vanilla extract
and milk.

Spoon the mixture into the petits fours cases, then bake
in the preheated oven for about 15 minutes until risen
and golden and the tops spring back when gently pressed.
Transfer to a wire rack to cool.

To decorate, divide the chocolate among three heatproof
bowls and set over pans of gently simmering water. Do not
let the bowls touch the water. Leave until almost melted.
Leave to cool slightly, then stir a couple of drops of green
food colouring into one bowl and a couple of drops of pink
into another. Leave the third bowl of chocolate plain.

Spoon white chocolate over four of the cakes, pink over
another four and green over the remaining four, then top
each one with a candy. Serve while the chocolate is still
soft, or leave to set and package up as a gift.

60 g unsalted butter,
at room temperature

60 g caster sugar

1 egg, beaten

60 g self-raising flour

¼ teaspoon vanilla extract

1 tablespoon full-fat milk

TO DECORATE

60 g white chocolate,
chopped

green and pink food
colouring

12 pastel-coloured
candies, such as jelly beans

*a 12-hole mini-cupcake
tin lined with petits fours cases*

MAKES 12

THESE PRETTY-AS-A-PICTURE LEMON SPONGES WITH A
CREAM CHEESE FROSTING ARE PERFECT FOR SERVING
AT CHRISTENINGS OR ANY NEW BABY CELEBRATION.

New Baby!

115 g unsalted butter,
at room temperature

115 g caster sugar

2 eggs

115 g self-raising flour

1½ teaspoons finely grated
lemon zest

TO DECORATE

115 g cream cheese

75 g icing sugar, sifted

1¼ teaspoons freshly
squeezed lemon juice

pink and/or blue food
colouring, as desired

edible silver balls

*two 12-hole mini-cupcake tins,
lined with petits fours cases*

MAKES 24

Preheat the oven to 180°C (350°F) Gas 4.

Beat the butter and sugar until pale and fluffy, then beat in
the eggs, one at a time. Sift the flour into the mixture and
fold in, then stir in the lemon zest.

Spoon the mixture into the petits fours cases, then bake in
the preheated oven for about 15 minutes until risen and
golden and a skewer inserted in the centre comes out clean.
Transfer to a wire rack to cool completely.

To decorate, beat the cream cheese briefly until soft.
Gradually beat in the sugar until smooth and creamy, then
stir in the lemon juice. Divide the frosting among two bowls,
add a few drops of food colouring to each one and stir well
to make pastel pink and blue. (Alternatively use the single
colour of your choice.) Swirl the frosting on top of the
cakes, then sprinkle over the silver balls.

DELICATELY SCENTED WITH ROSEWATER AND EACH
TOPPED WITH A SUGARED PETAL, THESE ELEGANT
CUPCAKES MAKE THE PERFECT TEATIME INDULGENCE
FOR MUM ON HER SPECIAL DAY.

Mother's Day

Preheat the oven to 180°C (350°F) Gas 4.

Beat the butter and sugar together in a bowl until pale and
fluffy, then beat in the eggs, one at a time. Sift the flour into
the mixture and fold in, then stir in the rosewater.

Spoon the mixture into the paper cases and bake in the
preheated oven for about 17 minutes until risen and golden
and a skewer inserted in the centre comes out clean. Transfer
to a wire rack to cool.

To decorate, brush each rose petal with egg white, then
sprinkle with the caster sugar and leave to dry for about
1 hour.

Put 1½ tablespoons lemon juice in a bowl, then sift the
icing sugar into the bowl and stir until smooth. Add a little
more lemon juice as required to make a smooth, spoonable
icing. Add one or two drops of food colouring to achieve
a pale pink icing, then spread over the cakes. Top each one
with a sugared rose petal. Leave to set before serving.

115 g unsalted butter,
at room temperature

115 g caster sugar

2 eggs

115 g self-raising flour

1 tablespoon rosewater

TO DECORATE

12 pink rose petals

1 egg white, beaten

1 tablespoon caster sugar

1½–2 tablespoons freshly
squeezed lemon juice

145 g icing sugar, sifted

pink food colouring

*a 12-hole cupcake tin,
lined with paper cases*

MAKES 12

115 g unsalted butter,
at room temperature

100 g caster sugar

2 eggs

115 g self-raising flour

3 tablespoons cocoa powder

3 tablespoons full-fat milk

25 g white chocolate chips

50 g mini-marshmallows

25 g flaked almonds or
slivered brazil nuts

TO DECORATE

100 g dark chocolate,
finely chopped

100 ml double cream

25 g flaked almonds or
slivered brazil nuts

25 g white chocolate chips

mini-marshmallows

*a 12-hole cupcake tin,
lined with paper cases*

MAKES 12

Father's Day

THE WINNING COMBINATION OF CHOCOLATE CHIPS,
MINI MARSHMALLOWS AND NUTS IN THESE 'ROCKY ROAD'
STYLE CUPCAKES IS GUARANTEED TO BE A HIT WITH DADS
EVERYWHERE – ESPECIALLY THOSE WITH A SWEET TOOTH!

Preheat the oven to 180°C (350°F) Gas 4.

Beat the butter and sugar together in a bowl until pale and
fluffy, then beat in the eggs, one at a time. Sift the flour and
cocoa powder into the mixture and fold in. Stir in the milk,
followed by the chocolate chips, marshmallows and nuts.

Spoon the mixture into the paper cases and bake in the
preheated oven for about 18 minutes until risen and the
tops spring back when lightly pressed. Transfer to a wire
rack to cool.

To decorate, put the chocolate in a heatproof bowl. Heat the
cream in a saucepan until almost boiling, then pour over the
chocolate and leave to melt for about 5 minutes. Stir until
smooth and creamy, then leave to cool for about 30 minutes
until thick and glossy.

Spread the chocolate mixture over the cakes and sprinkle
with the nuts, chocolate chips and marshmallows.

THESE ADORABLE FLOWER CAKES MAKE THE PERFECT
TREAT FOR GRANDPARENTS AND THE RECIPE IS EASY
ENOUGH FOR CHILDREN TO FOLLOW WITH SUPERVISION.
THEY'RE SO PRETTY NOBODY IN THE FAMILY WILL BE
ABLE TO RESIST STEALING ONE OR TWO!

Grandparent's Day

Preheat the oven to 180°C (350°F) Gas 4.

Beat the butter and sugar together in a bowl until pale and
fluffy, then beat in the eggs, one at a time. Sift the flour into
the mixture and fold in, then stir in the lemon zest.

Spoon the mixture into the paper cases and bake in the
preheated oven for about 18 minutes until risen and golden
and a skewer inserted in the centre comes out clean. Transfer
to a wire rack to cool.

To decorate, put the sugar and lemon juice in a bowl and
stir together until smooth and creamy. It should be thick and
spoonable, but not too runny. Divide the icing among two
bowls, add a few drops of food colouring to each one and
stir well to make a good vibrant pink and green.

Spoon the icing onto the cakes, allowing it to spread slightly
so that it resembles flower petals, then drop a sugar rosette
into the centre of each flower.

115 g unsalted butter,
at room temperature

115 g caster sugar

2 eggs

115 g self-raising flour

finely grated zest of 1 lemon

TO DECORATE

150 g icing sugar, sifted

1–1½ tablespoons freshly
squeezed lemon juice

pink and green food
colouring (or any colours
of your choice)

12 sugar rosettes

*a 12-hole cupcake tin,
lined with paper cases*

MAKES 12

115 g caster sugar

¼ teaspoon dried
lavender flowers

115 g unsalted butter,
at room temperature

2 eggs

115 g self-raising flour

2 tablespoons full-fat milk

TO DECORATE

185 g icing sugar, sifted

1 egg white

lilac food colouring

12 sprigs of fresh lavender

*a 12-hole cupcake tin,
lined with paper cases*

MAKES 12

SUBTLY FLAVOURED WITH LAVENDER FLOWERS, THESE
ELEGANT, GOLDEN CUPCAKES ARE PERFECT FOR SERVING
MID-AFTERNOON WITH A NICE CUP OF TEA. THEIR
OLD-STYLE CHARM MAKES THEM THE PERFECT TREAT
FOR A MUCH-LOVED GRANDMA OR GREAT AUNT.

A Treat for Grandma

Preheat the oven to 180°C (350°F) Gas 4.

Put the sugar and lavender flowers in a food processor and
process briefly to combine. Tip the lavender sugar into a
bowl with the butter and beat together until pale and fluffy.

Beat the eggs into the butter mixture, one at a time, then
sift in the flour and fold in. Stir in the milk.

Spoon the mixture into the paper cases. Bake in the
preheated oven for about 18 minutes until risen and golden
and a skewer inserted in the centre comes out clean. Transfer
to a wire rack to cool.

To decorate, gradually beat the icing sugar into the egg
white in a bowl, then add a few drops of food colouring
and stir to achieve a lavender-coloured icing. Spoon the
icing over the cakes, then top each one with a sprig of
fresh lavender. Leave to set before serving or packing.

A Surprise for Grandpa

DENSE AND ALMONDY WITH A STICKY, CHEWY MARZIPAN
CENTRE, THESE CUPCAKES ARE REMINISCENT OF A
TRADITIONAL BAKEWELL TART. PACK A FEW IN A TIN AS
A SURPRISE GIFT FOR A SWEET-TOOTHED GRANDPA OR
GREAT UNCLE AND WATCH THEM DISAPPEAR IN NO TIME.

Preheat the oven to 180°C (350°F) Gas 4.

Beat the butter and sugar together in a bowl until pale
and fluffy, then beat in the eggs, one at a time. Sift the
flour into the mixture and fold in, along with the ground
almonds and glacé cherries.

Spoon small dollops of the mixture into the paper cases,
sprinkle over some marzipan and top with the remaining
mixture. Bake in the preheated oven for about 18 minutes
until risen and golden and a skewer inserted in the centre
comes out clean. Transfer to a wire rack to cool.

To decorate, put the lemon juice and icing sugar in a bowl
and stir until smooth and creamy. Spoon on top of the cakes
and top each one with half a glacé cherry. Leave to set
before serving or packing.

115 g unsalted butter,
at room temperature

115 g caster sugar

2 eggs

100 g self-raising flour

40 g ground almonds

60 g glacé cherries, quartered

25 g marzipan, finely grated

TO DECORATE

2 tablespoons freshly
squeezed lemon juice

200 g icing sugar, sifted

6 glacé cherries, halved

*a 12-hole cupcake tin,
lined with paper cases*

MAKES 12

JUST FOR YOU!

Get Well Soon

LIGHT-AS-A-FEATHER GENOESE SPONGE TOPPED WITH
COOL CREAM AND NUTRITIOUS FRESH BERRIES MIGHT
BE JUST THE THING TO PERK UP A FRIEND WHO'S BEEN
FEELING UNDER THE WEATHER.

Preheat the oven to 180°C (350°F) Gas 4.

Put the eggs and sugar in a large bowl and whisk for about
10 minutes until thick and pale. Add the vanilla extract. Sift
the flour into a separate bowl twice, then sift into the egg
mixture and fold in.

Spoon the mixture into the paper cases and bake in the
preheated oven for about 12 minutes until risen and golden
and a skewer inserted in the centre comes out clean. Transfer
to a wire rack to cool.

To decorate, whip the cream in a bowl until it stands in
peaks, then swirl over the cakes. Top with fresh berries,
dust with icing sugar and serve.

Note: As these cakes don't contain any fat they don't keep
well and are best eaten on the day they are made.

2 eggs

60 g caster sugar

1 teaspoon vanilla extract

90 g plain flour

TO DECORATE

180 ml double cream

250 g fresh summer
berries, such as strawberries,
blueberries, raspberries
and redcurrants

icing sugar, for dusting

*a 12-hole cupcake tin,
lined with paper cases*

MAKES 12

For a Great Teacher!

115 g unsalted butter,
at room temperature

115 g caster sugar

2 eggs

115 g self-raising flour

115 g dried apple or
pineapple rings,
finely chopped

TO DECORATE

50 g ready-to-roll
fondant icing

yellow and green food
colouring

150 g mascarpone

50 g icing sugar, sifted

1 teaspoon apple juice

blue food colouring

*a 12-hole cupcake tin,
lined with paper cases*

mini-number cookie cutters

MAKES 12

WHAT BETTER WAY TO SAY THANK YOU TO A FAVOURITE
TEACHER AT THE END OF TERM THAN TO BAKE A BATCH
OF THESE CUTE APPLE-FLAVOURED CUPCAKES.

Make the number decorations the day before you plan to
bake the cakes. Divide the fondant icing into two pieces.
Add a couple of drops of yellow food colouring to one
piece and green to the other and knead until the colours
are well blended. Roll out each piece between two sheets
of greaseproof paper or clingfilm to 3 mm thick. Stamp out
numbers using the cookie cutters. Leave to dry overnight.

Preheat the oven to 180°C (350°F) Gas 4.

Beat the butter and sugar together until pale and fluffy, then
beat in the eggs, one at a time. Sift the flour into the mixture
and fold in, then stir in the dried apple pieces.

Spoon the mixture into the paper cases and bake in the
preheated oven for 17 minutes until risen and golden and
a skewer inserted in the centre comes out clean. Transfer
to a wire rack to cool.

To decorate, put the mascarpone, sugar and apple juice in
a bowl and beat together until smooth. Add a few drops of
blue food colouring and mix well. Spread the frosting on
top of the cakes and stick the numbers into the icing.

A Job Well Done

PACKED WITH COCONUT AND TANGY LIME, THESE
DELICIOUS CAKES WITH THEIR SNOWY-WHITE, RUFFLED
TOPS ARE EASY TO MAKE YET LOOK VERY IMPRESSIVE.
BAKE A BATCH AND OFFER THEM TO YOUR COLLEAGUES
TO ENJOY DURING THEIR TEA BREAK.

Preheat the oven to 180°C (350°F) Gas 4

Beat the butter, creamed coconut and sugar together in
a bowl until pale and fluffy, then beat in the eggs, one at
a time. Sift the flour and baking powder into the mixture
and fold in, then stir in the desiccated coconut and lime
zest, followed by the milk.

Spoon the mixture into the paper cases, then bake in the
preheated oven for about 17 minutes until risen and golden
and a skewer inserted in the centre comes out clean. Transfer
to a wire rack to cool.

To decorate, beat the cream cheese, sugar and lime juice
together in a bowl. Swirl the frosting on top of the cakes,
then sprinkle over the coconut shavings in a thick layer.

90 g unsalted butter,
at room temperature

25 g creamed coconut

115 g caster sugar

2 eggs

100 g self-raising flour

1 teaspoon baking powder

25 g desiccated coconut

grated zest of 1 lime

2 tablespoons full-fat milk

TO DECORATE

150 g cream cheese

50 g icing sugar, sifted

2 teaspoons freshly
squeezed lime juice

40 g coconut shavings
(moist not desiccated)

*a 12-hole cupcake tin,
lined with paper cases*

MAKES 12

100 g soft brown sugar

160 ml sunflower oil

2 eggs

grated zest of 1 orange

seeds from 5 cardamom
pods, crushed

½ teaspoon ground ginger

200 g self-raising flour

about 150 g carrot, grated

60 g shelled walnuts
or pecan nuts,
roughly chopped

TO DECORATE

150 g mascarpone

finely grated zest of
1 orange

1½ teaspoons freshly
squeezed lemon juice

50 g icing sugar, sifted

*a 12-hole cupcake tin,
lined with paper cases*

MAKES 12

You're a Good Neighbour

LIGHTLY SPICED AND TOPPED WITH A CREAMY CITRUS
FROSTING, THESE TASTY CARROT CAKES ARE JUST THE
THING TO TAKE ROUND TO YOUR NEIGHBOUR TO
SAY THANK YOU FOR ALWAYS BEING THERE TO LEND
A HELPING HAND.

Preheat the oven to 180°C (350°F) Gas 4.

Put the sugar in a bowl and break up using the back of a
fork, then beat in the oil and eggs. Stir in the orange zest,
crushed cardamom seeds and ginger, then sift the flour into
the mixture and fold in, followed by the carrot and nuts.

Spoon the mixture into the paper cases and bake in the
preheated oven for about 20 minutes until risen and a
skewer inserted in the centre comes out clean. Transfer
to a wire rack to cool.

To decorate, beat the mascarpone, orange zest, lemon juice
and sugar together in a bowl and spread over the cakes.

THESE MARBLED CHOCOLATE CAKES WITH A FEATHERED
CREAM CHEESE AND CARAMEL FROSTING ARE SMART
AND INDULGENT. TAKE THEM TO FRIENDS NEXT TIME
YOU'RE INVITED TO DINNER AND ENJOY THEM AS DESSERT.

Thanks for Having Us

Preheat the oven to 180°C (350°F) Gas 4.

Beat the butter and sugar together in a bowl until pale and
fluffy, then beat in the eggs, one at a time. Sift the flour into
the mixture and fold in, then divide the mixture between
two bowls. Add the cocoa powder to one bowl and stir in.

Drop alternating teaspoonfuls of the two cake mixtures into
the paper cases. Using a skewer, cut through the mixture
a couple of times to marble it, then bake the cakes in the
preheated oven for 17 minutes until risen and golden and
a skewer inserted in the centre comes out clean. Transfer
to a wire rack to cool.

To decorate, put the cream cheese and sugar in a bowl
and beat together until smooth and creamy, then stir in
the cream to make a smooth, creamy frosting. Spread the
frosting over the cakes, then squirt lines of dulce de leche
over the top. Leave as they are, or draw a skewer through
the dulce de leche to give a feathered effect.

115 g unsalted butter,
at room temperature

115 g caster sugar

2 eggs

115 g self-raising flour

1 tablespoon cocoa powder

TO DECORATE

150 g cream cheese

50 g icing sugar, sifted

2 tablespoons double cream

dulce de leche, for drizzling

*a 12-hole cupcake tin,
lined with paper cases*

MAKES 12

Index